The

JAZZ FLY

Starring

THE JAZZ BUGS

The Jazz Fly   Willie the Worm   Nancy the Gnat   Sammy the Centipede

Written and performed by Matthew Gollub
Illustrated by Karen Hanke

Tortuga Press Santa Rosa, California

Printed in China

Book design by Karen Hanke
Book production by The Kids At Our House
Musical score arranged by Aida de Arteaga

The artwork in *The Jazz Fly* was rendered as traditional pencil
sketches which were scanned and re-created on a Macintosh computer
using Adobe Illustrator. Musical narration of *The Jazz Fly* available online.

Publisher's Cataloging-in-Publication Data
(Prepared by Quality Books, Inc.)

Gollub, Matthew.
    The jazz fly / written and performed by Matthew
Gollub ; illustrated by Karen Hanke. – 1st ed.
    p.   cm.
    SUMMARY: Seeking directions to town, a fly
picks up the rhythm of the answers he gets from a
frog, a hog, a donkey and a dog, and then uses
these sounds to jazz up his band's music.
    "Starring the Jazz Bugs: the Jazz Fly, Willie
the Worm, Nancy the Gnat, Sammy the Centipede."
    LCCN: 99-94968
    HC ISBN: 978-1889910-17-8   PB ISBN: 978-1889910-43-7
    PB Special Edition (without CD) ISBN: 978-1-889910-47-5

    1. Jazz–Juvenile fiction. 2. Flies–Juvenile
fiction. 3. Musicians–Juvenile fiction.
I. Hanke, Karen. II. Title.

(HC) 15 14 13 12
(PB) 10 9 8 7 6 5 4 3 2 1
(PB Special Edition) 10 9 8 7 6 5 4 3 2 1

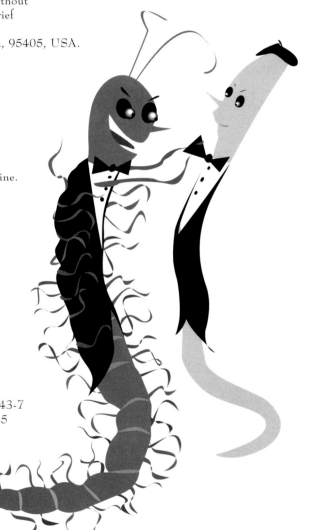

*To my family, and to children everywhere who
have learned to speak a second language.*
– M.G.

*For my mom and in memory of my dad.
And with love to Bob, Kris, Becky and Dr. Brown.*
– K.H.

ZZZ...ZZZ...

A fly buzzed by.
It was late in the day,
and he was lost.

So he flew to a frog
that was sittin' on a log
and asked the frog
which way to town.

"*ZA-baza, BOO-zaba, ZEE-zah RO-ni?*"
The frog didn't get the way the Jazz Fly talked.

"RRRibit," the frog answered.
"Rrribit. Rrribit!"

The fly flew – *zzz* – to a hog in a bog.
He stayed clear of the mud to keep his black tux clean,
and asked the hog which way to town.

"ZA-baza, BOO-zaba, ZEE-zah RO-ni?"

"Oink!" the hog answered. "Oink! "Oink! OINK!"

The fly saw a donkey short and gray,
so he flew – *zzz* – to ask *him* the way.
"ZA-baza, BOO-zaba, ZEE-zah RO-ni?"

The donkey just began to bray.

At last the fly flew to a furry dog.
One…more…time…he asked,
"ZA-baza, BOO-zaba, ZEE-zah RO-ni?"

"Rruff!
Rruff! Rruff!"

barked the pooch right away.
She pointed her nose to say,
"Go that way!"

The Jazz Fly flew past weeds and clover
till he reached a street that was paved all over.
He leaned left down the alley,

right through the door.
He saw fancy waiters creepin'
all across the floor.

Beetles and maggots had come to hear the show.
They were dining with the locusts by the fireflies' glow.
The band was lookin' antsy. It was half past eight.
They grumbled, "Man, this fly is always late!"
The fly tugged at his sleeves, strolled to his drums,
twirled around his brushes and counted off a song:
"ZA...ZEE...
ZA-zee-ZOO-zay!"

Willie the Worm inched
up and down his bass:
*Bi-BIM-bum
BOM-bum,
BIM-BIM-bum
BOM-bum...*

Nancy the Gnat sashayed with her sax: *NREE...NA na noo na. NREE... NA nu na-na nay...*

Sammy the Centipede hit
the piano keys
like a man
with a hundred hands:
DAH-DEE
boogie woogie woogie
DAH-DEE boogie
DAH-DEE-woogie
DAH...DEE!

The fly swished with his brushes...

Swish!

Thump!

thumped his bass drum...

made his cymbals ring:

Zing! Ving! Ping! Fing!

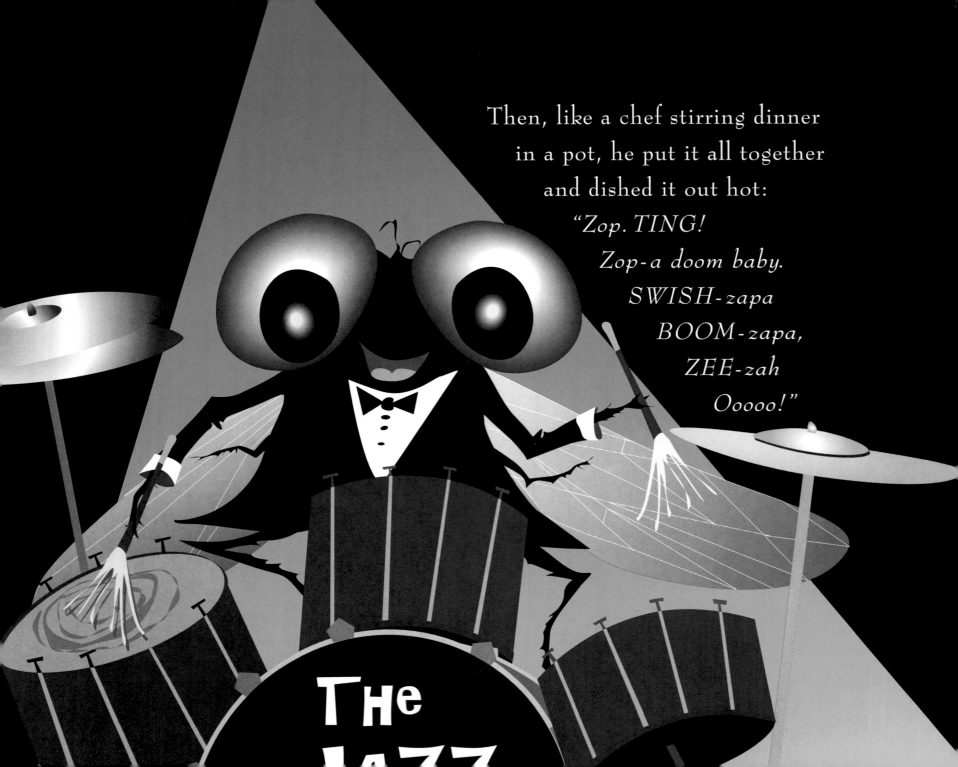

Then, like a chef stirring dinner in a pot, he put it all together and dished it out hot:
"Zop. TING!
Zop-a doom baby.
SWISH-zapa
BOOM-zapa,
ZEE-zah
Ooooo!"

The fly was jammin'!
Not scammin'.
But swimmin'
like a salmon.

But then the club's Queen Bee
sat down with a huff:
"This band plays good
but that's not enough.
I want a sound
that'll make bugs shout.

I want a new BEAT
or this band is OUT!"

The fly, who'd been very confident until now,
suddenly felt kind of
small.
He knew he'd have to come up
with something different
if the Jazz Bugs were to keep
their jobs at the jazz club.

So he thought...and thought...until...

...The fly recalled the sounds he had heard that day.
He mixed 'em all up in a brand new way!
He crossed a bridge, stepped beyond the line,
took a chance and began to shine:

"Swish zoom zoppety-boop...

ZOPPEDY-dome bang...

RRIBIT, RRIBIT!

Swish-zab zapa zapa...

OINK! OINK!

Zuba, ruba,

HEE-HAW-HEE!

RUFF RUFF RUFF!

Za-ba-da da-ba-da da-ba-da da-ba-da

HEE-HAWroni!

OINK za-ba

HEE-HAW RRIBIT RUFF TING!"

Well, the beetles
and the maggots
stopped eatin'
their chow.

Willie and Nancy
and Sammy said,
"WOW!"

The cockroach waiters shouted,
"Go, man, go!
Dig that fly,
he can really blow!"

The joint was hoppin', boppin',
wrigglin' on the floor.
They'd never heard a sound
like this before!
Now word got out 'bout the Jazz Bugs'
sound, 'bout the white hot drummer
who broke new ground.
Beetles packed the club.
Locusts came by swarm.
The Jazz Bugs' names went
UP in **LIGHTS**.

And to make sure he
never again lost his way,
the fly...picked up his friends...
in a limo each day!

Author's Note

Many different experiences inspired this story, including the countless times I've lost my way in foreign countries. I just seem to entertain my very best daydreams while the required bus, train, oxcart, camel, or ferry comes and goes. Then I must ask local bystanders for directions. Most people in foreign countries, however, do *not* speak English, so this calls for some of what I consider the three i's: ingenuity, improvisation, and interpretation.

Ingenuity can mean simply using the right words at the right time. Even a stilted phrase in a foreign language such as "Next bus when?" may be quite ingenious if it communicates your point. When you improvise, you create something at the moment with what's available. Using your day pack to keep your hair dry when you don't have an umbrella is improvising. When you interpret, you convey something that you perceive in your own way. Paint the sky purple instead of blue and you're interpreting. Perhaps more than any other art form, jazz honors the three i's, the abilities that make each of us a unique human being.

The jazz phrasing found throughout this story (ZA-baza, BOO-zaba, ZEE-zah RO-ni, for example) is based on a type of singing called scatting. Early African-American musicians first applied scatting to jazz. Scatting picks up where language leaves off, communicating feelings and nuances that words alone cannot express.

You may notice that some lines in this story rhyme and some don't. I purposely selected the non-rhyming words for their bounce and the mood they convey. If you'd like to read *The Jazz Fly* as it sounds on the CD, listen for the accents and count 1-2-3-4. Each **bold** word below falls on either 1 or 3:

1   2   3   4   1   2   3   4

Zzz ... *Zzz* ... A **fly** buzzed **by**. It was

1 2   3   4 1 2 3 4

late in the **day**, and **he** was **lost**. So he...

But don't feel bound to the way I recite the story. Play with the phrases. Acquaint them with your mouth. Introduce the words and rhythms to your friends. With time, perhaps in the spirit of jazz, you'll take the language in a direction all your own.

– M.G.